# Between Here and Home

Matt Daly

# Between Here and Home

Matt Daly

Attention schools and businesses: for discounted copies on large
orders, please contact the publisher directly.

For information contact:
Unsolicited Press
Portland, Oregon
www.unsolicitedpress.com
orders@unsolicitedpress.com
619-354-8005

Cover Design: Kathryn Gerhardt
Editor: S.R. Stewart

ISBN: 978-1-950730-04-9

# Table of Contents

# Characters

PAM, late 30s, not yet an alcoholic but she is on her way, never told anyone but the warden himself that she was once pregnant with his child, drives herself home from the Campfire Tavern regardless of her condition

BERTIE, ghost of Skylar's mother, loved to dance

BEV, owner of the Campfire Tavern, Bertie's lifelong friend, skeptical of newcomers and some old-timers

SKYLAR, early 20s, Bertie's son, an addict, knows more than he lets on

RUSS, Skylar's father (unacknowledged), keeps his distance from Skylar at Bertie's request, keeps his chest pains to himself, sometimes with Janie, a fisherman

JANIE, sculptor, artist, sometimes with Russ, an observer

RICHARD, retired doctor, inherited the ranch once belonging to his wife (unnamed) when she died with no other heir

BUDDY, old friend of Russ, Bev, and Bertie, drives himself home from the diversion dam regardless of his condition

THE WARDEN, Pam's lover before he left town, a stranger

DEER, here before the town, casualties

RIVER, unobstructed from its source until the dam east of town diverts most of the water for irrigation

WIND, unobstructed or at least indifferent to obstructions

HIGHWAY, a danger to those crossing and to those following its passage

# Prologue

# The Campfire Tavern

-

East of town, the cliffs have a broken-nose look.
Summer thunderstorms punch them hard and quick.

-

Bev watches the weather change from behind the bar.
Just a few tables have chairs facing the window.

-

Janie joins Russ in his booth.
They brush knees under the table.

-

Richard sees some faces in the mirror have a sunken-eyed look.
He wears a white mustache groomed in a Civil War style.

-

Skylar watches his own reflection in the mirror behind the bar.
He is pretty sure Russ is keeping an eye out for him.

-

Buddy hasn't been in for a while.
He must be back to drinking out by the diversion dam.

-

Pam jingles her keys in her hand.
She thinks she's earned the coin she flips.

-

Bev keeps most of what she notices to herself.
She knows a thing or two about chance.

-

Outside, sagebrush collects what the wind carries.
Deer don't pay much mind to what tangles in the branches.

-

Bertie looked pretty rough before the lung cancer took her.
Nobody outside her family ever called her Roberta.

-

Bev keeps a picture of Bertie from high school taped to a mirror.
She looks at it when she cuts lemons.

-

Richard usually sits alone at the bar.
He and his wife never once came to the Campfire together.

-

Bertie & Bev ran around with Russ & Buddy in their youth.
They were together that time Russ's car went end over end.

-

Bertie told Bev everything there was to say about Russ.
Long before the swell in her belly gave her away, Bertie
whispered, *Sky.*

-

Russ has been giving his LPs away one paper bagful at a time.
Near the end, he and Bertie danced a time or two to slow songs.

-

Bertie raised Skylar on her own.
She never would say who the father was.

-

Janie does not like to talk about her artwork.
She harvests hawk feathers and cottonwood bark over by the
cemetery.

-

Richard visits Janie's website more and more.
He is thinking about installing one of her sculptures in his yard.

-

Pam gets Richard's name wrong.
Most everybody notices but no one corrects her.

-

The game warden left quicker than most.
Driving, Pam rolls up her window when she thinks of him.

-

These days, Russ's van tops out at thirty-five.
He spends a lot of time rattling over the rumble strip.

-

Russ feels shooting pains in his arm sometimes.
He thinks the river is his secret to give away.

-

Buddy's beer hand is missing its ring finger.
It's for the best he is not making any big plans.

13

-

Methamphetamine has the same future for Skylar as anyone.
Hanging out by the KOA near the oxbow is not going to help.

-

Pam figures she's not the only one with a secret.
She wonders if anyone else keeps one in a drawer by the bed.

-

After fishing, Russ sometimes stops by Janie's studio.
She likes the sound of his watch ticking on her nightstand.

-

No one, not even Russ, asks if Pam is okay to drive.
He nurses diet soda in his booth by the door.

-

Janie knows exactly what Bev thinks of her.
The line of Bev's mouth says it all.

-

Bev quit driving by her family's homestead years ago.
She visits Bertie's grave every Sunday.

\-

Pam has seen Richard fixing fences at his wife's place.
Deer leap easily over the wires.

\-

Russ and Janie think the same thing when Pam stumbles out.
Bev whispers under her breath.

\-

Richard sees Pam's truck reflected in the mirror.
He recalls the feel of a dead woman's hand.

\-

It is not just Pam and Buddy betting against the wind.
The wind never makes a friendly wager with anyone.

\-

Deer come into the cut pastures at sunset.
Sooner or later everybody hits one between here and home.

\-

# 1

# Post-Anesthesia: Pam After the Wreck

Is this how

it feels          to become

                    a ghost?


Is this how

it felt

                    the needle?


I feel

this white          sheet

        but beneath

parts          of me

                    and the feeling?


        Where          is everything

I am          used to

                    feeling?


          She is this          white

                    I feel

beneath                    the sheet.


          This is her

teaching          me

          to be          a ghost.

# Richard Reads the Aeneid

I found comfort once, in days when I had no name,
reading of Aeneas founding Rome. With my blood
on both palms, I pulled wire for my wife, stung again
and again by the strung barbs. I penned mares and foals,
separated them with driven posts, unspooled wire.
She watched from the window when the foals nursed. I stayed
as silent as the child we knew would never grow
inside her, like a bronze blade whetted between us,
splitting us in two.

Now I visit Pamela, pulled from the wreckage
of roadside phlox, shooting stars, plastic trash, and sage.
I wash my hands before touching her wrist. Pam lies
under the same cold bulbs that never dimmed that night
my wife was lost at last to that knot no scalpel
could split from her bones, I feel an ancient song rise
in me. Some survive, like the tyrant Metabus,
buried deep within Virgil's catalogs of names,
ancestors of the enemies of Aeneas
from the olive-sided hills he was prophesied
to steal.

Names, native-born, whose lives Virgil muscled through lines
before his hero dispatched them. Metabus fierce,
a warrior, who carried his infant daughter,
Camilla, as he fled. His people had risen
against him. His enemies displaced him from his

throne, hunted his blood, her blood. Camilla swaddled
in rough linen, a seed destined to be armored,
quivered, slain. Metabus crouched low in thickets, wails
from his bundle masked by the roar of the deluge
he knew he would somehow have to cross.

His enemies closing in, he ripped rags to cinch
the child to his spear shaft, then cast her over those
full waters to drown in their rush or pierce the loam
of pastures his bloody hands had not subdued. Just
a river could be the break between this cruel life
and another life. And here, all of us hefting
our own burden: Pamela's life. Our indifference
to what we knew would come of her behind the wheel
was as sharp as any spear cast not over far
Amasenus's banks, but into floods of wind
over the dry pasture.

Each of us begins, a curl in a liquid world.
Together we lofted Pamela across, knew
no one strikes that far bank without the binding cords
cinching tight enough to cut through flesh. We know each
of us must ford that current, either lose ourselves
in the torrent or sink, lost at last among mares,
on an unknown shore. We hunt riverbanks clouded
with leafless branches for a gap to cast our spears
and the burdens, loved and ignored, we have bound there.
Each of us a bloody tyrant.

## Buddy's Drinking Hand

Didn't know I was missing one
'til after. Not when I woke up in a ditch,
spinning wheels, shattered glass, little rocks. Not
when I crawled off in the red clay wash, looked
up through the animal night at stars chucked
across the sky. Not even after I woke up again,
head caught between chunks of sandstone
and the splitting maul of the sun. Wasn't
'til I made it over to Bev's (was it Bertie's?)
that I saw what I'd done.

Past what should have been
lunchtime, when those rotten bluff sides go
flat bright, whoever it was creaked hinges
on the screen door, taped over with a split
grocery sack to stop some wind, looked straight
down to my side, *Where's your goddamn finger,*
*Buddy? Got it in that pocket? Never get that*
*bloodstain out now, Buddy. It's all soaked in.*
Then the other one started in, *Saw cop lights*
*a while after you left us. Knew it'd be you, Buddy.*
*Should have listened. Should have stayed put.*
Then me, *Can't change what's done, ladies.*
*That finger's long gone now.*

Swear I still feel it grip the side
of one of those cold bottles Bev probably still
swings down the bar. Haven't been in to see her
in more months than I want to count. Never did

hold Bertie's hand in her bright metal bed
or go see her in her grave.

# Skylar Found an Arrowhead

Messing around
by those river cliffs
across from the KOA,
just messing around
like a kid, I was
a kid, throwing rocks
at trees, at birds
at whatever I thought
       I could hurt.

I almost skipped
the arrowhead
over the water
before I felt the edge-
black nick my finger.

On the ride back,
it poked my leg
from where it sat
inside my jeans pocket.
With every pedal,
it poked. I left it
       on the table
       by Mom's bed,

if that's what you call
the place they lay you

out on your way
to being dead. I told her
it would protect her,
       its darkness
against the deeper dark.

Just last week,
I broke the tip off
prying at the back
of the watch she gave me,
       messing around
       with the watch
       she gave me.

I scattered
some gears, springs
that fell out,
into the river.
It didn't matter
those parts went
missing. I'd given up
telling time.

# Russs Sings on the Rumble Strip

Makes little sense to Janie why I drive this way.
She doesn't know the way I get when people push.
She doesn't know what can rattle out on highways,
how, at its edges, pavement crumbles into dirt.

She doesn't know what can happen in the river
when I feel currents break apart and fill back in.
Makes no sense to her why I just keep on trying
to rumble some rusted part loose from this old van.

This driving side of me once made sense to Bertie.
She knew just what to say to keep me on the road.
I've lost so much by driving down this old highway
like snowmelt runoff rushing past the stone I carved.

# Janie's Nocturne

His watch on my nightstand ticks me awake
to a waterlight moon. I step barefoot
into hoarfrost on the new deck, ice-strewn
by banked clouds eddying western ridges.

My toes shimmer at the edge where shadow
touches gleam. Crystals glint like lawn fairies
my child eyes saw when leaves and vapor met.
Between the Hunter's belt and the moon's face,

one cottonwood rises bare. One black, curved
night hunter lifts its sextant wing, pursues
phases of the horizon. Deck boards pop
under my heels. Blue hands of winter creep
up these fish-patterned pajamas I gave
Russ to fill my nightstand empty as sky.

## Bev Cutting Lemons

I keep Bertie's old bowl full of lemons
in front of my favorite picture of her.
Bertie puckering a kiss for the camera
with Russ behind the lens. Just blue
all around her. Just us and all that
open ground. No storm yet. No shadow.

Two slices in Bertie's rum and Diet Pepsi.
One wedge in Grandma's Tab
as regular as English tea.

Some hot days, Janie comes in early
from collecting feathers, whatever else
the gusts bring her. She's the only one
who wants tea with lemon. I give her
the old bags with leaves turned to dust.

Wind has worked cracks into my fingertips.
Splits I have not yet noticed sting
where the juice drips in. Bertie watches
from her frame. I am past
the need for wincing.

Richard says it might be
Pam wakes up today. I ought to go over
visit her, what's left.

# Russ Eases the Way

I remember that first time Pam walked
in with the warden. They broke through the shade
of the old doors together, laughing
in a way that made me start too.
I hadn't heard a word of what passed
between them, him still in his red uniform shirt,
her shaking her hair out of her ball cap.

I laughed along with them and they noticed
and didn't mind at all. What I felt
was about Bertie and me before I let all that go
to hell and knew I'd made it so. I let myself
feel the old way and laugh. I liked how I felt
watching Pam come in, watching how
after a while, she went out with her warden.

Sunlight can come into the Campfire Tavern
brighter than halogen. Some afternoons it spots
every mote kicked up to either get breathed in
or to settle dingy on a picture frame, harsh
enough to yellow the memories fixed under glass.
But that day all it did was fall down
all around Pam while she was laughing.

# Fawn Before Highway

tall     grass     golden

sharp     purple     thistle

ears     prick     swivel


stumps     string     ribbons

bright     thorns     tangle


loud     roars     racing

path     shards     pebble


young     legs     spraddle

firm     land     clatters

wind     leaps     under


teeth     shine     silver

eyes     screech     over

clover     crushes    odor

outside     bodies    crumple

inside    bodies   crumple

# 11

# Bev Finds the Ultrasound

Pam's little place was tidier
than I expected: how white
she kept the walls, how light
fell through windowpanes,
to her side table, her polished stones.

Houseplants needed water
so I watered them. On the sill
in her bedroom, I watered them,
plucked a yellow leaf or two.

I saw it when I sought a place
to put the leaves, a book for her
to read, a snapshot to look at
as she learned about life
with those dead legs.

Nightstand drawer slid
open like it was waxed. Inside
a white figure curled
in a black bowl.

Where did she put that shape
once growing inside her?
When did she choose a life
with the child removed?

I held up that lone image,
Pam's baby in one hand,
tin watering can loose in the other.

Sunshine lit a glass of water full
of little bubbles. After
I closed the empty drawer,
I went to the store
to buy her magazines, to ask
if anyone remembered.

# Russ Remembers His First Close Call

I used to drive fast all the time, faster
drinking. I was with Bertie and Bev
the first time it cost me, headed back
from the Palmer place. Last time Bev
let Bertie bring me to the family homestead.
Bev used to think the old place was all right
for drinking. Used to be we all agreed.
My old sedan, the kind of deal I could pick up
off rodeo cowboys before all their hard luck
drained into the night, hit a rut wrong
on a rise. We lifted, delicate as dubbing
and hackle swung in a tight loop over a river
seam. Worn out shocks gave such a softness
to the ride none of us noticed we had left
the ground until we hit it again. All three of us
in the front seat. Behind us the empty night
we were always running from. Headlights
shot wild at horizon, gravel, sky. Back then
if you landed upright and nothing was broken,
you put it back in gear. None of us knew
Bertie had my boy inside her.

# Skylar's Tooth

It's not a baby
tooth. Just one
no other pushed
out of my head.

Dentist called it
an eye tooth.
Said he'd cap it
to look like all
the rest.

      Mom called it
      a reminder
      but never did
      say of what.

When she got sick,
I thought
I looked tough
sucking my tongue
through the space
it made.

Kids learned quick
what they'd get
for pointing
out the gap

that showed
the odd times
I'd smile.

Mom made Russ
go fish with me
to talk tough
and trouble.

He showed me
his bridge, all
those teeth, fake
in his mouth,
like we shared
some secret.

Russ said
he'd come close
to the edge. His
eyes flashed
like mine.

I've thought
about a bridge
for my bottom teeth
I've lost
this year.

I get tired
of Bev saying

I look just
like mom.

Now that she's
underneath,
I'm nobody's
baby.

# Buddy Has Words With Skylar

"You look like your mother," I tell him
whenever I see him up here or down lower
by the KOA. "What's it to you, bud?" Not knowing
he uses my name. "There's nothing to it," I want to say
to him but never do, "Not a goddamn thing to it.
Just an observation I thought you might like,
you stupid son-of-a-bitch."
                    But I do not say that or anything more
than, "Never mind." I just like to think of her
when I see him, thought he might want to think of her.
          "Well, bud, you look like a fucking raven
with that shiny can gripped in your claw."
Him sitting there on a cement table at the rest stop
across the parking lot from the diversion dam.
"You're right about that, boy," I say
as I take a long pull from the can. "Who you calling *boy*?"
He goes red. So I fix him with that black-eyed stare
I learned from Russ but folks in town think must
be on account of something Indian. "You, *boy*,
that's what I'm calling you." Before the evening
gets away from us, the highway patrol cruiser
swoops in black and chases us both away.
          I feel like I run into him less and less
since those others showed up around the campground
since it got too wild down there for me. My stump
finger aches whenever I do see him. Every time,
I think of her when I see him.

# What Pam Knows

The way Bev worried
            her bottom lip
that first afternoon,

the way she bent
            to place the magazines
                        by my bedside,

I knew
*she knows.*

Even then
I would not pretend
            I was sleeping.

These days
she brings yellow tulips
            from the grocery.

Each time
            she ties them up
            with a ribbon
                        of a different color,

never red        or white.

In some of the tulips
    little black beetles
        scale the pistil.


    Maybe she thinks
I want to fill
        my emptiness.


      Each visit
    there is a moment
when I think      *here it comes.*


But then nothing,
    just a pause
        in her breathing.


She won't tell me.
She doesn't need to
    say a word.


    So she knows
        about the baby,
    what I chose
in a different life,


    when I had a life
        from the waist down.


At least I know
she can keep a woman's secret

if she cares to,

the way she keeps
        fallen leaves
                off Bertie's grave.

At least I know
        how over Bertie's secret
                *Russ and that boy*
she can still bend down
        deep and low.

# Deer Have a Mineral Hunger

hiss      of river      under wind

hiss      of movement      on ground

too hard      for earth


new grass      under peltgrass

summer fattens      spots away


new green      under      severed stems

we risk      against cold


wolves      never speak

of these killers      these eaters


we would not      believe them

if they spoke      to us

of killers      like these

sunrise    killers    spew minerals

under    flat haunches    without tails

we explode    before them

black birds    pick us apart

start anus    start eye

# Russ Fishes the Oxbow

By their choice or mine they come and go
like birds on wavelets, birds near the eddy's edge:
mallard, merganser, ouzel, gadwall. Some dip
under. All rise, eventually, gone to air. I watch
a kingfisher from where I stand in the back eddy
slack water, behind this boulder where I once tried
to carve her name. Kingfishers cut through currents
to minnows underneath, spear them with their beaks.
Bertie stood once where I stand now, pulled three fish
too big for an osprey to carry, much less a kingfisher:
rainbow, cutthroat, brown. Laughter and her singing
reel. Kingfishers laugh more often than they sing.

Some days I bring myself here to where currents
work away at where they touch rock, carvings
I made on the stone's surface growing smooth.
Some days, I don't even bother to string the rod
I bring down from the truck, my gesture
to the waterbirds, to the kingfisher perched
on her powerline, always with me, needed or no.

## Janie Finds Her Materials

Russ knows I combed the cemetery grove
for leaves edged like feathers, a deer's jawbone
today. I tell him I saw Bev there. She is
never too busy with Bertie's gravestone

to notice or with her eyes to opine. After dusk,
I tell Russ how Bev brushed away snow with her
ungloved hand. I tell him about the moon
cottonwood, gleam, and owl. His eyebrows twitch

when he smiles at these worlds we live beside.
Russ stands in my bedroom doorway, knee-deep
in pursuit of shadows on the river-
bed, banks rimed with the waning night's jetsam.
He knows what gifts I seek in rafts of clouds,
why I look to fill our unmapped spaces.

# Bev Remembers Cranes

Summers we searched for hatchlings
no taller than seed heads
in tall grass along the spring bottom.

I knew why you searched for them:
how you knew father cranes watched
over chicks as their down sloughed away,
how gray flight feathers followed brown.

You could tell mothers from fathers.
There was some small difference
you never shared that made you certain
which parent strode patiently before us,
croaked its alarm whenever one of us
cracked a stick beneath our feet.

Could you still spot the offspring
even after their feathers grew long
enough, gray enough to carry
their grown bodies out of sight,
past the downy summer clouds?

We lived with their migration.
For them, our place was a nesting place.

# III

# Russ Builds a Ramp for Pam

This ramp I hammer together
will get her past her columbine all gone
to seed, past what's left of her other flowers.
Once she rolls inside, she's on her own
for that other, harder getting past:
seeing sun touch everything, wondering
if it might still warm her skin (*how good
the sun still feels on my hands*).

The sun might just be strong enough to make
her wheel herself out past the threshold
to her garden to feel the wind brush columbine
petals across the palms of her hands. She could
come back down to the rest of us waiting
at the Campfire. That part's up to her.
Perhaps this ramp will ease the way.

# Bev Writes to the Warden, Then Russ

I.

Dear,

you son-of-a-bitch, she's a mess.     You left
Pam     a mess.
They found her in a ditch. You left     like the rest.

I believe you thought you could     leave
before she could no longer hide          disguise
what you left.  But I
I found     the film     she hid
in a drawer
in her dresser
by her goddamn bed.

She won't ever walk
again     you son-of-a-bitch.
You left. She traded     a wheel for a wheel
for a wheel. She traded     her life, that dear life
like a coin she thought she'd earned
her right     to flip.

I'll bring you     back
you son-of-a-bitch.     I can't
let you leave     your mess. I can't be

the one to clean up     this mess. You aren't
the only one who believed
after leaving,     *please*
*someone else*
     *clean up this mess.*

          You aren't the only one
          who ever left me a mess.


2.


Russ,   you dear, you son-of-a-bitch
You fled.   She hid.   She couldn't hide
from me or keep hidden     the mess you left
for me and the rest.

Now     the boy     he's a mess.
He still lives, just another     son-
of-a-bitch     goes on living.

          You     in the water.
          Her, just bones     in a bed.

## Janie Sees the Ultrasound

I never meant to see you, your cloud shape
residue, your pendulum swung across
that square of night paper creased to crosshairs.
Your nebula face lifted as if space

could be righted. I reached for a lemon,
Bev busy at the taps, and there you were.
Who bore you folded in her hip pocket?
And before, in her unlit depths, a mere

dream fire flickering inside her midnight
hopes? Why did Bev try to hide you between
Bertie, shining as if the cosmos did
not shadow her way, and the bowl she made?
I see each of your moon faces, lemons
from which I want to suck out all the sour.

# Russ Recounts His Second Close Call

Below zero, had to be. Ice crystals sparkled
on the street. Above, frozen pinpoints, like deer
eyes lit by headlights driving home. Me, steaming
hot, standing in the street. Buddy's words
about Bertie and me like match strikes in my ears.
In those days I was always on fire. Buddy,
not as soft as now, bare-chested, head against the curb,
lolling drunk. Dribbles of bloody slime froze his face
to the gutter. Me standing, boot raised over him,
his bare head. Clean sound in my ears,
like my hammer driving nails into the first
morning boards. Jumbled sounds from folks
who stumbled out to watch. From Bertie, cries
like a baby squalling. She helped me get my boot
heel down safe, to stay away long enough
to let the liquor and red heat drain away.

On cold nights now, Janie asleep with or without me,
all I have to listen to are logs ticking in the woodstove
in the walls as they settle. I remember Bertie's eyes
that night and one other night. She was right
to make me swear I'd stay away when the boy came
from her. She was right to say heat fills a space
whether we want it to or not.

# The Wind Does Not Sing to Skylar

I hear my mother
in the gust
come dancing
over the river flash.

Doesn't matter much
what she says.

Oxbow goes all full
of shimmer too bright
to see through
though I keep looking.

The others laugh
at my quiet, think
my eyes narrow
onto some other
vision. Someone sings.
Someone else joins in
but it would take
darkness for me
to follow them.

I squint until all I see
are sparkling pinpoints
and a greater lightness.

I listen, not to them
their singing songs
or to their laughter
but to the wind.

It's more than enough
to hear Mom's voice
again, though I can't
tell what she's saying.

## Dying Fawn

what is    inside is    outside now

red stain    red    stain red from pink

mouth    black already    birds    already many

black birds    blue-black birds    black-and-white

birds    already inside my red    inside    now outside

bird sounds    black eyes    grass sounds

sharp blades    cut stalks    outside the mouth

not inside    never inside    never grasses beyond

tall grasses    beyond    tall grasses

# Richard Delivers the Ultrasound

Bev nestled the envelope carefully within
the stack of bills by her paring knife, her lemons
in a glazed bowl she says Bertie made in high school.
Despite her effort to hide it, I could see it,
manila cradled by sheaves of white. Three words stamped
in red ink, "Do not bend," on the exposed corner.
I did not need to see the contents to be sure
of the contents. The address did not need to be
visible for me to know the destination.
That jutting point of golden paper smeared with red
said enough about her desperate throw, what she hoped
would lodge in the heart of the warden, a man whose
name was lost to most of us before he fled from
this landscape besieged.

"I will take them, your letters," and Bev accepted,
not knowing what Janie had told me she noticed
behind Bertie's photo, the one with the lovely
eyes, the fierceness, the face that said it would endure
even if she knew it would not. I do not know
why Janie told me, but I was happy to be
the one she told. I was happy to have her lean
so close, have her breath soft in my ear even if
there was only hardness to what she said. Her hand
gentle on the back of my hand, "Richard, what will
we do? Pam has lost so much, Richard, but how can
we know if some of what she lost she was ready

to let go? Should we let the warden know?"

Bertie's hand gripped my hand hard. Only once, before
she died, but tight as the talons of an osprey
grip the flesh of the flashing fish they hunt. So much
of Bertie lost its softness before she let go.
"I am worried about the boy, Richard. Skylar,
what he will do without family to hold onto."
"His father?" "His father." Her smile withered away
stiff as a knucklebone. "We all choose what we hold
onto, Richard, what we let go. I am worried,
Richard, Skylar won't let go."

Just now, the mail and that manilla envelope
on the bench seat beside me, "Do not bend." The day
warm enough to roll my window down. I finger
the corner dull, the red letters there. I pinch down
to the stiff film inside. Instead of town, I drive
down to the pasture where my wife's last horse grazes
the last of the soft grass pushing dry through the snow.
I hold the letter to the wind. I let it go.

# What Pam Does Not Say

"I'm tired," as I flop
       this limp stalk
              of me from bed
to chair. I do not say, "Today,

      I don't want to try
              to push myself around."

      Instead, I grip
the wheels outside
the tires,
      push my way
              down slick halls.

My nurse yawns
      into what's left
              of night. She trails
along. "How come," I say,
      "I don't think
              I've seen you

before?" She tells me,
      "Unless you're up
              at night, you won't see
                    me. I work
third shift. I know
      only night people."

I do not need
to ask her if
    *third shift* means
        the same as *graveyard*
or what she sees
    in the dark.

She leaves me
    when we reach
        the plate glass
windows. A gasp
    of night air
        when doors hiss
            open,

hiss closed. Lines of gray
    make a horizon. *Day people*
    is what I am now.

What I do not say,
    now that no one
        is here to listen
            is, "I want
a crescent moon
    to come
over the ridgeline.

I want to be me
    under white
        light. I want

to be warmed
by a campfire,
held in a curve
of stones I made
with black sides
facing the flames."

What I do not say
is, "Most flowers
planted outside
survive a night
or two of frost."

I do not say,
"I don't care
if a moon wanes
or waxes." Should I

stoke my fire to burn
hotter, burn
past the hard curve
I made? Or let it
sink back to black,
to a disc cooled
by dawn? What I do

not say is how
much I know
I will miss campfires,

how much the night.

# Russ in the Current

I feel a tingle run up my right arm
at each solid take, at the moment
each fish's taut charge pulses
up the line, piercing the skin
of the river, through the rod
and into me.

Charge flows in clear filament,
from the conductor lodged, a kite key,
in the cloud-white trout mouth
and beyond into the greater dynamo
of river flesh.

I stand in noonlost shadows now
cradling the wet reel. A sharper
twinge in my left hand narrows
my eyesight to the one bright pinprick
of that barbed hook cast out for me
fifty-one years ago.

# IV

# Deer Standing Before a Road-Killed Fawn

some of us       go

some       come back

never       come

back       some of us

cross over       never

cross over       never cross back

some cross over       some cross back

all of us       wonder

crossing       at coming back

all of us       flash white

crossing       some flash red

## Men Danced with Bertie

There are just three
reasons men ever danced
with me.     One: dreams
of closer. Two:  numb
to worse. Three:  not to say
goodbye. Palms hot
or cold, high on my back
or low      I danced full
arcs of stars to keep
their palms from balling
into fists. I stomped
hardwood until dawn      lit
up Bev's unwashed window-
panes. I would have      held
onto anyone      to keep me
from the day. One by one
they released me.      All
three released me. Russ
and Buddy circled      skin
to skin beside the curb. Loving
me enough      to throttle
one another all through
that longest night.      Skylar
even then hidden      inside
never once toddle-stepped
balancing on my toes
round      and round. *You will*

*lose everything,*    I never
let him know.

# Skylar Watches the Evening

I watch Russ fall
down in the riffle
where sun cracks
the surface. I see
him go
under the gleam.

My father
dead and gone.

I know something
about falling
into light
too bright
to see by

clear as glass
when you feel
too broke to fix.

Water all full
of shards.

# By Janie's Nightstand

"Pam's I bet," Russ said into the blue night
of my bed. My fingertips wove bird-shapes
beneath his collarbones. His voice trailed off
into moth wings searching out some brightness

to beat against. My birds became leaves, first
of cottonwoods then the Russian olives
he worried would choke all his riverbanks.
For him, words aloud formed their ideas.

For him, fish were still the river until
his hand on their white undersides raised them
from the water. I lifted myself, my
breasts on his chest-down, belly on his pale
belly, as if pressing skin against skin
could be more real in our night world than words.

## Pam's Mercy

1.
One last time
the nurse pushes me down
     one white corridor,
          another.

Her shoes
     squeak. My wheels
     squeak.
         The carpet hisses
             like little snakes.

2.
One time, before
the warden (Why won't I
     say his name?)
         knew the choice
     I made, he took me
to ride out
to check out
     a report
         of a poached deer.

His red shirt
     sleeve flapped.
     Wind rocketed past

71

his side mirror.

I kept my window up
    so I could hear
        him talk
    about mercy-killing deer
        hit on the highway
            left for dead
                but not dead.

When we reached
the body, a clean black
    hole above the hole
        where ravens plucked
            out the eye.

Warning sounds, dry
    from the viper hidden
        in the shadow cast
            by the dead deer's legs.

He dodged
    the strike, pressed
        his boot down
            on that snake's head
        until it squirmed
    itself rattledead.

Wind hissed all around
    me, feeling

                inside what was
                        never his:
        that girl shape
                I was growing inside,
                        that shape the world
                                would stomp out
                                        sooner or later.


3.
Down the last white hall,
        my feet in their braces,
                my hands grip the wheels.
                        I am able
                                to crash
                                but not to stumble.
                I cannot move now
                        any way but a clean line.

But I can last
        a little longer
                under the boot
                        of the world.

# Dirt Holds the Bones

(Buddy Read *Sometimes a Great Notion*)

           I remember reading that story
while my stub healed up, getting used to getting by
with one less. The book, by that acid trip guy
with the bus, about those loggers, whole family
up in the rain northwest of here. Old man loses
his arm somehow.
           Remember him dangling it out
the window, flipping the bird across that swollen
current churning against the foundation of the house
they tried to keep together against everything
carried by the water and everything else.
           Whole story starts with that dead arm
flipping off the world. I stole the library copy.
Thought I'd find acid trips, hippy girls, free love,
all of it. Just that arm sticks with me now.
           My finger is out there somewhere
by the red clay wash on that sharp bend, just bones,
like a little line of white rocks. Not hanging
from nothing, no house, no big bend in no big river
to wash its hanging place away. Still pointing
at all the people on the road.
           Big rivers must wash all the bones,
each and every one, all the way to the ocean.
Out here, dirt holds the bones. Each white line
points to some memory or to something lost.
Mine is out there telling whoever finds it
just how I have felt all along.

# Richard Shuts the Gate

I never figured out how to stop her brother
laughing at my city hands. I never puzzled
out why they used barbed wire to secure the barbed wire
gate, unless to test the limits of outside men.
For years my fingers were always nicked and bloodied
from thorned loops of wire holding each pasture gate shut.
Her brother drove and set most of the posts, dug most
of the post holes himself, strung most of the three strands
of barbed wire himself. At the far edge of the west
pasture he left a few of the posts suspended
in air, held by the tension in the wires. At each
gate, a heavier post pounded deep, looped bottom
and top with strands of barbs a little shorter. He
knew these loops were too short but strung them anyway.
They all did. Too short unless you had lived through taut
secrets of a life with cattle in a place where
wind was more constant even that work, than anger
at how the ends never quite met. I leaned with all
my weight, pushed with all my strength in one arm bundled
up close to my shoulder, reached and tugged at the wire
with the other, scraping the barbs over gray wood
weathered after one season in the wind. After
seasons in the wind, I knew they were laughing, not
showing me this meaningless little secret: how
to shut a barbed wire gate.
                                        The next day we get sun,
I'll put on my new work gloves, take nippers, a spool

of smooth wire, replace every loop at every gate.
I will remember how she looked, my wife, when he,
her brother, gave in to the softness we all give
in to, how soft his hands appeared, suspended there
between her calloused palms. Once I pluck those last thorns
looped just for me, I will be rid of him for good.

V

# Visions from the Diversion Dam

(Buddy Finds the Ultrasound)

                                        gusts
carry silver sounds hearts pulsing
canyons feeding the river its silt


                                        sunset
flashes a gold scrap over the sage
I track back to where it ripped free


                                        envelope
is a pocket big enough for an image
fetal form without the need to crease


                                        picture
sheltered out here black & white
among yellow flowers and bones


                                        flames
flared off last from the gas field
some places better left to the dark


                                        ghosts
find it hard to look into some faces
harder to get rid of some than others

# Skylar Counts Himself Among the Travelers

Osprey dive straight
down, no gliding
over the surface,
just straight into fish,
points of their claws
before their fierce eyes.

       I've heard people
       claim birds of prey
       sometimes can't
       unlock their talons.

Richard says he saw
one time on some trip,
fishing trip, to Canada
or something some eagle
locked dead in the back
of a big dead salmon.

       I used to think
       Richard's more full
       of shit than any
       of the rest of them.

Then yesterday
watching pelicans

soar white,
thinking how far
to any ocean,
an osprey dropped
like a knife.

Water in tears
fell from its body.
Whatever it grabbed
was too much
weight, pulled its white
struggle downstream.

I never saw the ocean,
not waves, not birds,
not white birds
over waves.

       All I've ever seen
       are waves of heat,
       sage rolling,
       wind to the horizon,
       pelicans black-edged
       above gusts.

       All I look for is ways,
       other ways than winged
       ways, to soar up,
       to dive under,
       what passes for air.

## Richard Keeping House

I chose the bowl with a rim of woven horsehair,
its impractical edge, not its utility
appealed to me. Some small impracticality
inside this coped-log order my wife's family left.
I am an unwitting steward. My skin still flushed
where Janie's fingers brushed my wrist as she settled
the bowl into my palms.

Dare I believe she was more pleased with the buyer
than the sale? This vessel of braided willow she
harvested in winter, when wind sears all exposed
skin red, now resting here, on a pine hutch shelf warmed
by windowshine and the woodstove's cast iron.

I stare into the spiraling fibers. The old
stove ticking from coals as if fall had already
pulled air too tight for warmth to perch on its fine strands
and horses all rimed from each other's breath standing
tail-whipped to the wind. This stove my wife's brother knew
I could not ignite without smoking up the room
and was wrong.

The bowl on the empty shelf where my wife tossed keys,
mail, newspaper coupons she sometimes used. The bowl
holding dawn in its shallow curve. I wish Janie
could stand here when the dawn first comes in, warmth pouring
past the edge she wove for me. But I remember

Russ gone to the river, his death an ancient sort
of leaving, proper for him, and for me beyond
hope. My talent is for lasting.

I long for Janie here, my arms around her,
a spearpoint of light piercing the backs of my hands
cupped over her middle. I wonder what she might
say if she could see this place, what I have made it
despite the curvature, we assume of stories
lost to inheritance or less. I long for her,
in my wife's old house, with the shapes I trust, the sounds
of cold horses seeping under the front door warp
I never intend to plane.

# Bev Clears Snow

Last night's wind did most of the work,
left a hard crumb crust against the line
where we sunk Bertie's gravestone. No name
for the place where trunk becomes root.

I wonder if she can still feel our gusts
through the side of the bluff, tickling
chokecherry roots Russ chose
to plant. Wind crawls under my gloves.

It's not a bad day to clear snow
from her resting place, sun on its low arc.
Cold burns my cheeks a little,
red like the night Skylar was born.

I don't have the heart to tell her
how ragged the chokecherry looks
after these last few easy winters.

She knows though the boys seem lost
to us, all come to rest beside us,
soon or even sooner.

# Pay Me a Visit

(Bertie's Wish)

Russ never did
not after I told
him     no visit
hospital     house
hospital     here
he did     what I said
he should     do

Buddy lived
through his losses
he did     what I said
he should do

Richard knew
my voice     how
it could make
boys pull apart     what
it could make
boys do     he held
on to me     when
he let me     go

my boy lived too
let me go, boys,
let go     too

# Skylar Holds His Mother's Picture

I should leave
what's left of it
under that tree
Bev worries over.

      But then Bev will know
      I've carried it
      here in my pocket
      all this time.

She might decide
to carry it herself.
      But time's come
      to let go.

Come morning,
this will all be
lost in the dawn
east of me.
Like the sun
I'll keep on to the west
watching all the green
and the rivers grow.

Where the waters
join in darkness,
I'll fold up what's left

of my only picture
of my mother
       Roberta.

It won't be a song
I sing when I place
her in the obsidian
ocean, just the tide.

It won't be the wind
then but fierce sounds
       of distant birds.

## Pam Replants Her Garden

I insisted on paying Bev
    for the dirt she brought over.
    The unopened sack drooped
        over its own middle fold,
        reminded me of me now,
chair-me. I couldn't stand
looking at that goddamned bag,
    slumped away from siding
    and my cinderblock foundation,
        so I wheeled down the ramp to put
        the soil the bag held in the ground.

I put in columbine for Russ,
or for what he is now—
    man-in-the-grave. I'll give
    them to Bev when they bloom
        to put with him, to pay him
        what I can for this ramp
            he hammered together,
        the gift he left here for me.

For Bev, a few sunflowers
    to cut before they sag,
    big and full of seeds.
        Something for her to take
        to Bertie where she tends her.

I mixed that new dirt
with the old, thought
    of planting myself
    a wild rose but I've been around
        long enough to know underground
        they tangle every other root
            they touch. Their blossoms
            are pretty when they flash
                but the rest of them
                gets in the way.

I'll wait to plant
anything for me, to see
    what can best stand
    the dry and cold and still show
        buds like little embers
        glowing night or day,
what bears the warmth that sends
some bolting past the weight
    of themselves, their stems
    can carry. I'll leave an empty pot
        by where this ramp now covers
        where stairs used to be.

# Materials for an Armillary Sphere

|                       |                              |
|-----------------------|------------------------------|
| cliff rock            | face of a gibbous moon       |
| river stones          | some cleave-sided            |
| flint shards          | knapped to a point           |
| kingfisher feathers   | other feathers               |
| deer antlers          | matched pairs, many sizes    |
| glazed bowl           | inverted and opaque          |
| hinges                | rusted from screen doors     |
| engine parts          | gears of many sizes          |
| barbed wire           | a little, like everything    |
| cottonwood branches   | soaked and shaped            |
| plant stalks          | dried sunflowers             |
| mud tiles             | stamped with other flowers   |
| tall grass            | places for everything to spin |
| wind                  | let up from time to time     |

# Acknowledgements

First and always, I am grateful to my family. Cindy and Frank, I love you.

Heartfelt gratitude to the poets and writers who gave their time and attention to helping this book find its way, especially Laurie Kutchins, my most skillful guide. Thanks to Lucy Flood for friendship, advice, and laughter throughout the process. Thanks to Bethany Schultz Hurst, Connie Wieneke, Susan Austin, George Vlastos, and to my sister, Meg Daly, for close reading, skillful critique, and encouragement.

Many other writers and editors contributed to this work. Cheers to them all. In imagining a community I found a real one.

The team at Unsolicited Press has been fantastic. S. R. Stewart's editorial advice made the book better.

My poet-brothers Eric Paul Shaffer and Jose A. Alcantara keep me going and push me to be better. I hope I can do the same.

*Richard Shuts the Gate* was published in the anthology *Blood, Water, Wind, and Stone: An Anthology of Wyoming Writers*, published by Sastrugi Press.

*Bev Clears Snow* was published in The Cortland Review's Issue 70.

Previous versions of three poems: *Russ in His Favorite Back Eddy, Russ Remembers His First Close Call,* and *Russ Recounts*

*His Second Close Call* were published in Split Rock Review's Issue 4.

*Russ Builds a Ramp for Pam, Russ Sings on the Rumble Strip,* and *Russ Remembers His First Close Call* were read for the Wyoming Public Radio podcast *Spoken Words*.

# About the Author

Matt Daly teaches reflective and creative writing to people of many ages and professions. He collaborates regularly with visual, performing, and literary artists on indoor and outdoor exhibitions of text-based work. Matt has received a Neltje Blanchan Award for writing inspired by the natural world and a Creative Writing Fellowship in Poetry from the Wyoming Arts Council. He is a resident faculty member at the Jackson Hole Writers Conference. He lives in Wyoming with his wife and son.

## About the Press

Unsolicited Press got its start in 2012 in California and is now based in Portland, Oregon. The press publishes exemplary poetry, fiction, and creative nonfiction from emerging and award-winning writers around the world.

Learn more at www.unsolicitedpress.com.

CPSIA information can be obtained
at www.ICGtesting.com
Printed in the USA
LVHW031734030619
619985LV00003B/742/P

9 781950 730049